On the Go
Trucks in Action

David and Penny Glover

PowerKiDS
press.

New York

Published in 2008 by The Rosen Publishing Group, Inc.
29 East 21st Street, New York, NY 10010

First Edition

Editor: Camilla Lloyd
Editorial Assistant: Katie Powell
Designer: Elaine Wilkinson
Picture Researcher: Diana Morris

Picture Credits:
The author and publisher would like to thank the following for allowing these
pictures to be reproduced in this publication:
Cover: Christine Osbourne/Corbis, JCB; Jacques Jangoux/Alamy: 4, PB
Galleries/Alamy: 22; Alan Schein/Corbis: 1, 6, Dave G. Houser/Corbis: 9t, Vince
Streano/Corbis: 14b, Corbis: 11, 13t, 13c, 18, Patrick Bennett/Corbis: 12b, Helen
King/Corbis: 14t, George Hall/Corbis: 15, Christine Osbourne/Corbis: 16, Lester
Lefkowitz/Corbis: 17, Valentin A. Enrique/Sygma/Corbis: 19, Duomo/Corbis: 20,
Bettmann/Corbis: 21; Juan Silva/Image Bank/Getty Images: 5, Walter
Hodges/Stone/Getty Images: 7, 8, Mitch Kezar/Stone /Getty Images: 10; JCB: 12t;
John Callan/Shout Picture Library: 9c.
With special thanks to JCB.

Library of Congress Cataloging-in-Publication Data

Glover, David, 1953 Sept. 4-
   Trucks in action / David and Penny Glover.
      p. cm. — (On the go)
   Includes index.
   ISBN 978-1-4042-4310-1 (library binding)
   1. Trucks—Juvenile literature. I. Glover, Penny. II. Title.
   TL230.15.G583 2006
   629.224—dc22

                              2007032247

Manufactured in China

Contents

What are trucks?

Trucks are vehicles that carry **loads**. A big road truck may carry food, furniture, and other things. This truck is carrying tree trunks.

load

A forklift truck moves loads in a factory. The driver slides the fork under the load, and then lifts it into place. This forklift truck is lifting and moving boxes.

box

fork

Truck quiz
What does a forklift truck do?

Truck parts

The front part of the truck is called the **tractor**. This is where the driver sits in the **cab**. The tractor has an **engine**. The tractor pulls the **trailer.**

cab

trailer

tractor

wheels

The trailer carries the load. It does not have an engine. Its wheels turn as the tractor pulls it.

This is an **articulated truck**.
It bends when it turns a corner.
The truck can have one or
more trailers.

Truck quiz
Which part of a
truck has an engine?

What is inside?

The driver turns the steering wheel to steer the truck. His cab is high up, so he has a good view. The driver uses the gearshift to go at different speeds.

speedometer

steering wheel

gearshift

This trailer is called a **Winnebago**. It is a traveling home. Inside there are beds, cupboards, a kitchen, and a bathroom. There is even a TV inside!

Truck quiz

What does the gearshift do?

What makes it go?

engine

The truck's engine makes it go.
It turns the wheels to pull the
truck along. The engine is in
the tractor underneath the cab.
The engine runs on **diesel fuel**.

The truck's wheels turn on **axles**. Axles are rods that fix the wheels to the truck's body. The wheels have thick, rubber tires to grip the road.

axle

wheel

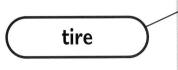

tire

Truck quiz
What fuel does a truck engine use?

Working trucks

Dump truck

A dump truck is very tough. It carries soil and rocks. The trailer tilts up to dump the load.

load

trailer

trash can

Garbage truck

A garbage truck lifts and tilts the cans. Then a **crusher** squashes the trash down.

Breakdown truck

A breakdown truck has a **winch**. The winch pulls the car onto the ramp.

ramp

winch

Truck quiz

Which truck has a crusher?
What does it do?

Special trucks

Car carrier truck

Some trucks are made to carry special loads or do special jobs. This **car carrier truck** carries cars.

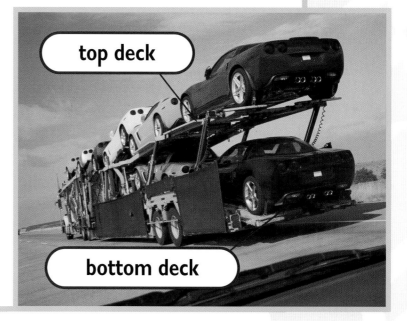

top deck

bottom deck

drum

Cement mixer truck

It carries wet cement in its giant drum.

Ladder truck

Firefighters use a ladder truck to fight a fire in a tall building. The hoses squirt water into the flames to put out the fire.

ladder

hose

Truck quiz
What does a cement truck carry in its drum?

Record breakers

Road trains are the longest trucks in the world. They travel on long, straight roads across Australia and the United States. This road train has three trailers.

tractor

trailers

Giant dump trucks are the heaviest trucks in the world. They work in quarries and mines.

This giant dump truck could carry a whole house in its huge trailer. Its wheels are twice as tall as a man.

Truck quiz

Which countries have the longest trucks in the world?

Driving safely

A truck driver must be careful and drive safely. He must always wear a seatbelt and watch the road ahead. The driver checks his mirrors before **passing**. If there are no other vehicles coming, it is safe to pull out.

mirror

headlights

flashing turn signal lights

At night, the truck's headlights light up the road. The driver can see what's ahead. Other drivers can see the truck coming. Flashing turn signal lights show that the truck is turning.

Truck quiz

How do you know if a truck is turning?

Truck fun

Trucks take part in competitions and shows. A monster truck has huge wheels on a small body. It can drive over a pile of old cars.

flatbed trailer

A truck with a flatbed trailer makes a good parade float. The parade team decorate their float and dress in colorful costumes.

Truck quiz

What kind of truck trailer makes a good parade float?

Old trucks

This truck is one hundred years old. The first trucks were powered by **steam engines**. The truck driver puts coal on a fire in the engine, to keep the truck going.

Truck words

articulated truck
A truck that bends between the tractor and trailer.

axle
The rod through the center of a wheel.

cab
The part of the truck in which the driver sits.

car carrier truck
A truck with two levels for carrying loads. Car carriers are double-deckers.

crusher
The part of a garbage truck that squashes the trash.

diesel
The fuel a truck engine uses to make it go.

engine
The part of the tractor that makes it move.

fuel
Something that burns inside an engine to make it work.

load
The things that the truck carries from place to place.

passing
When one vehicle goes past another on the road.

steam engine
An engine that works by using steam.

tractor
The front part of the truck that pulls the trailer.

trailer
The part of the truck that carries the load.

winch
A part that winds up a wire to pull up a load.

Winnebago
A trailer that can be used as a traveling home.

Quiz answers

Page 5 A forklift truck moves loads in factories.

Page 7 The tractor.

Page 9 It makes the truck go at different speeds.

Page 11 Diesel fuel.

Page 13 A garbage truck. It squashes the trash down.

Page 15 Wet cement.

Page 17 Australia and the United States.

Page 19 Its turn signal lights flash.

Page 21 A flatbed trailer.

Index

Web Sites
Due to the changing nature of Internet links, PowerKids Press has developed an online list of Web sites related to the subject of this book. This site is regularly updated. Please use this link to access this list:
www.powerkidslinks.com/otg/trucks